Explaining Covenants

Tom Marshall

Sovereign World

Sovereign World Ltd
PO Box 777
Tonbridge
Kent, TN11 0ZS
United Kingdom

Series editor: Susan Cuthbert

Unless otherwise indicated, all scripture quotations are from the New International Version, inclusive language version, copyright the International Bible Society 1999; published by Hodder and Stoughton.

ISBN: 1 85240 347 0

The publishers aim to produce books which will help to extend and build up the Kingdom of God. We do not necessarily agree with every view expressed by the author, or with every interpretation of Scripture expressed. We expect each reader to make their judgment in the light of their own understanding of God's Word and in an attitude of Christian love and fellowship.

Cover design by CCD, www.ccdgroup.co.uk
Typeset by CRB Associates, Reepham, Norfolk
Printed in the United States of America

Contents

Introduction

What is a covenant?

The concept of covenant is central to the whole divine revelation that comes to us through the scriptures. Indeed, it is not overstating the case to say that biblical religion is always covenant religion.

Our Bible is divided into the Old and New Testaments, that is, the old and new covenants, and Sunday by Sunday at the communion service we repeat the words of Jesus, *"This cup is the new covenant in my blood"* (1 Corinthians 11:25).

Yet if the truth be known, most of us have very little knowledge of what a covenant is. We may have a vague idea that it is something like a legal contract, a pact or a will. Nevertheless, covenant is not a term that enters very much into our modern vocabulary.

However, grasping the true nature and significance of covenant will unlock the meaning of many passages of scripture, and will transform our understanding of the nature of our relationship with God through Jesus Christ, our Lord. That is the theme and purpose of this present study.

1

The nature of covenant

The motive for covenant: relationship

The origin and heart of all covenants is that they have to do with God's relationship with all people. Human beings alone were created with the unique capacity for relationship with their Creator. The Bible therefore defines us not as the end result of an evolutionary process, but in terms of our relationship with God: *"God created human beings in his own image"* (Genesis 1:27).

We begin therefore with this fundamental key to understanding all the biblical covenants.

▶ *Covenants spring from God's desire to have a relationship of personal intimacy with people.*

This central emphasis on relationships as the reason behind covenant is clearly expressed in the three-part covenant formula recurring throughout scripture:

> *I will be your God* (Genesis 17:7–8)
> *You shall be my people* (Exodus 6:7)
> *I will dwell in the midst of you* (Exodus 29:45–46)

Wherever this formula is found, either in part or in full, the context is always covenant. For example:

> *I will walk among you and be your God, and you will be my people.* (Leviticus 26:12)

The same theme can also be found in Genesis 17:7; Exodus 6:7; Deuteronomy 29:12–15; Jeremiah 31:33; 32:38; Ezekiel 27:27; Zechariah 8:8; 2 Corinthians 6:16; and Revelation 21:3–7.

The covenant relationship

Here is another fundamental principle of covenant:

▶ **The relationship in covenant is a bonded one, requiring commitment or personal loyalty.**

The Hebrew word for "covenant" is *b'riyth*, meaning "to bind." Therefore a covenant is not merely a personal relationship, even an intimate one; it is based on a solemn promise and confirmed with an oath.

The bond that a covenant creates between two parties makes them one. Thus we read that *"Jonathan became one in spirit with David"* (1 Samuel 18:1), or as the Revised Standard Version puts it, the soul of Jonathan was *"knit"* to the soul of David. Genesis 2:24 tells us that a man will be *"united with his wife, and they will become one flesh."*

The bond that covenant creates between two parties is therefore:

1. **Pre-eminent**, that is, its obligations supersede and take priority over all other claims.

2. **Permanent**, that is, it is not time-based or for a limited period. Covenants are therefore perpetual or everlasting.

3. **Inviolable**, that is, kept sacred or secured from violation. Because of the sacred nature of the covenant bond, to break it is, in God's eyes, the most serious kind of wrongdoing imaginable.

God's covenants with people

When we consider the covenants that God has made with his people during human history, we will find from first to last that *relationship* lies at their heart. In fact, every permanent relationship between God and human beings is based on covenant.

The covenant in Eden
Although the term "covenant" is not used in the first chapters of Genesis, it is clear that God had a covenantal relationship with Adam and Eve in the garden of Eden. God was their God, they were his people and God walked with them in the garden.

It was also a relationship of great personal intimacy. God put Adam in the garden, and instructed him to take care of it. God gave him commands to obey, and brought the beasts and the birds for him to classify and name. Moreover, God was close enough to Adam to see his inner aloneness, and made the woman to be his helper. What is more, God personally introduced Eve to Adam (Genesis 2:15–22).

When Adam and Eve sinned, they broke covenant.

> *Like Adam, they have broken the covenant –*
> *they were unfaithful to me there.*   (Hosea 6:7)

Rejecting the obedience of living in personal intimacy with the Creator and instead seeking independence and autonomy, Adam and Eve suffered the inescapable consequences. They were expelled from the garden, and for the first time felt the pain of mortality and a terrible spiritual aloneness. No initiative on their part could ever find the way back to the tree of life (Genesis 3:24).

Nevertheless, it was there that God's redemptive search to restore the broken relationship with his people began. This restoration is also expressed in the form of covenants.

The covenant with Noah
The first time the word "covenant" appears in scripture is in God's promise to Noah, *"I will establish my covenant with you"* (Genesis 6:18; 9:8–16). But already the emphasis is on relationships, for concerning Noah we read that he *"found favor in the eyes of the LORD"* and *"was a righteous man, blameless among the people of his time, and he walked with God"* (Genesis 6:8, 9).

To the Hebrews, righteousness has always been a relationship term. It means maintaining the covenant.

The covenant with Abraham
One of the pivotal passages in the Old Testament is God's

covenant with Abraham (Genesis 15:8–21, 17:1–22), to which we will return later in this study. We have God's own endorsement of Abraham:

> *But you, O Israel, my servant,*
> *Jacob, whom I have chosen,*
> *you descendents of Abraham my friend.* (Isaiah 41:8)

> *Abraham believed God, and it was credited to him as right-eousness, and he was called God's friend.* (James 2:23)

The covenant with Israel

This covenant was mediated through Moses, with whom God spoke *"face to face, as one speaks to a friend"* (Exodus 33:11). Deuteronomy 4:37 tells us that it was make with Israel because God *"loved your ancestors and chose their descendents after them."* Henceforth, just as human beings were defined at creation in terms of their relationship with God, so now Israel as a nation became defined in terms of its covenant relationship with God.

> *For you are a people holy to the LORD your God. The LORD your God has chosen you out of all the peoples on the face of the earth to be his people, his treasured possession.* (Deuteronomy 7:6)

The covenant with David

The covenant made with David ranked in importance with the Abrahamic covenant and was exceeded in significance only by the new covenant foretold by Jeremiah. Again the key was intimacy with God, for God described David as *"a man after his own heart"* (1 Samuel 13:14), and said:

> *He will call out to me, "You are my Father,*
> *my God, the Rock my Savior." . . .*
> *I will maintain my love to him for ever,*
> *and my covenant with him will not fail.* (Psalm 89:26, 28)

The new covenant

In the new covenant, foretold by the prophets and accomplished through the death and resurrection of Jesus Christ, our lost relationship with God is finally restored. Now we, Jew and

Gentile alike, are the Israel of God, his covenant people. Our corporate identity, like that of Israel, is established by the covenant.

> *But you are a chosen people, a royal priesthood a holy nation, a people belonging to God, that you may declare the praises of him who called you out of darkness into his wonderful light.*
>
> (1 Peter 2:9)

But individually we also, like Abraham, Moses and David, become God's intimate friends:

> *"You are my friends if you do what I command. I no longer call you servants, because servants do not know their master's business. Instead, I have called you friends, for everything that I learned from my Father I have made known to you."*
>
> (John 15:14–15)

This is the final covenant between God and human beings. There will never be another, nor will another ever be needed, because this one leads on to the finally perfected restoration of relationships in the New Jerusalem.

> *And I heard a loud voice from the throne saying, "Now the dwelling of God is with human beings, and he will live with them. They will be his people, and God himself will be with them and be their God."*   (Revelation 21:3)

How covenant arises

We come now to some other important characteristics of covenants between God and human beings. These affect the entire nature of the covenant relationship.

▶   **A covenant is not an agreement between parties of equal standing and power, but between unequals, the initiative being taken by the stronger party, who voluntarily binds himself to take on an obligation to the weaker party.**

In the covenants between God and people, the initiative is

always taken solely by God. The Bible never records examples of people proposing covenants with God; it is always God who offers his covenant to people.

> *"I will establish my covenant as an everlasting covenant between me and you and your descendents after you for the generations to come, to be your God and the God of your descendents after you."* (Genesis 17:7)

> *"The time is coming," declares the LORD,*
>   *"when I will make a new covenant*
> *with the house of Israel*
>   *and with the house of Judah."* (Jeremiah 31:31)

▶ **Because the covenant is God's initiative and God's gift to us, it is founded by grace. It is also maintained by grace and it operates solely on the basis of grace.**

That means that the covenant relationship:

1. **Is completely undeserved and unmerited**, that is, there is no virtue or worthiness on our part that gives us any claim on God's attention.

2. **Is actually an expression of generous and forgiving love** on the part of God against whom we have offended and sinned.

3. **Does not spring out of any need on God's part** to have a relationship with human beings or to have our fellowship. It is the free and sovereign expression of the graciousness of his character.

It is noteworthy that it is in the context of the covenant that God's character is most fully revealed, as it was to Moses:

> *And he [God] passed in front of Moses, proclaiming, "The LORD, the LORD, the compassionate and gracious God, slow to anger, abounding in love and faithfulness, maintaining love to thousands, and forgiving wickedness, rebellion and sin."*
> (Exodus 34:6–7)

Here is a sevenfold cluster of divine attributes – compassion, graciousness, patience, loving-kindness, truth, faithfulness and mercy. At the heart of them all is *hesed*, the word invariably used in the Old Testament when speaking of the love of God. *Hesed*, sometimes translated "loving kindness" or "steadfast love" or "everlasting kindness," is faithfulness to the covenant bond.

> *Know therefore that the* Lord *your God is God; he is the faithful God, keeping his covenant of love* [hesed] *to a thousand generations of those who love him and keep his commands.*
> (Deuteronomy 7:9)

▶ **In a covenant, it is the stronger party who sets out the conditions under which the covenant obligations will be fulfilled. In covenants between God and human beings, God alone sets the terms.**

Thus, while a covenant is an agreement between two parties, it is an agreement only in the sense that the recipient, the weaker party, must agree to the terms given in order to participate in the covenant.

In the covenants between God and people, it is always God who makes the covenant and who sets the terms. God offers his covenant to us and we can accept it or reject it, but the terms are never open for debate. They are not subject to negotiation.

> *Then he* [Moses] *took the Book of the Covenant and read it to the people. They responded, "We will do everything the* Lord *has said; we will obey."* (Exodus 24:7)

This is a very important principle to understand when we come to discuss the terms of the new covenant. One of the real reasons why so many of us do not experience the blessings of the covenant is that we have considered the terms too demanding. Therefore, we have either tried to side-step them, or have tried offering God some alternatives that are more acceptable to us.

▶ **Because the covenant deals with God's relationship with human beings, it is all-embracing. No part of a person's life is outside the covenant.**

The covenant began in Eden, in God's personal relationship with Adam and Eve. It covered the totality of their life: physical, moral, spiritual, intellectual, emotional, vocational and relational. It will end in the renewed creation as God dwells fully with human beings. This is the ultimate and eternal goal of God's covenant:

> *Now the dwelling of God is with human beings, and he will live with them. They will be his people, and God himself will be with them and be their God.* (Revelation 21:3)

Thus, God's covenant relationship always extends to every domain of human life. It brings every sphere of human activity within its scope: temporal and eternal, spiritual and secular, individual and societal, private and public, personal and institutional.

▶ **Finally, covenant must also enable people to live in relationship with a holy God.**

For the covenant relationship to be totally restored, God sought:

1. **A final resolution of the problem of sin**, one that would fully satisfy both his holiness and his mercy, and

2. **A final resolution of the problem of obedience**, so that people could live in harmony with the law of God – the terms of the covenant.

As we will see, this is the supreme provision of the New Covenant sealed in the blood of Christ.

2

The nature of the covenant bond

We have already seen that a covenant is the most serious and solemn of all relationships. Now we have to understand why that is so – why God takes it so seriously.

There are three major steps involved in making a covenant:

1. **A promise**

2. **An oath**

3. **A sacrifice.**

Promise – the commitment of covenant

People nowadays make promises very lightly and break them with little compunction. Because of that we have virtually ceased to consider a promise to be of any consequence, and this is one of the main reasons why we have difficulty trusting God's promises. We don't take promise keeping very seriously ourselves, and find it hard to believe that anyone else, even God, would be really meticulous about keeping his promises.

We need to understand what is meant by a promise and why it is binding. What actually happens when we make a promise? What happens when God makes a promise?

A promise is generally an undertaking to do or to give something in the future, or to refrain from doing or giving something in the future. But a promise is not merely a proposal or an intention:

1. **It is a serious and earnest commitment** as to how we will act in the future, and

2.   **It is intended to be relied on** as an assurance that we will, in fact, act in the way we have declared.

3.   **It also means that we take on the obligation to fulfill our pledged word** when the time comes, no matter how costly or inconvenient it may be to do so. In other words, we limit our freedom of action in that particular situation, because we consider ourselves duty-bound to act or do exactly as we have said.

God takes his promises very seriously. When he makes a promise he has committed himself to that course of action, and we are meant to take the promise as a guarantee that he will do exactly as he has said. Moreover, when God makes a promise he limits his sovereignty or freedom of action. He has thereby bound himself in advance as to what he will do in certain situations, and he cannot do otherwise.

> *Know therefore that the LORD your God is God; he is the faithful God, keeping his covenant of love to a thousand generations of those who love him and keep his commands.*
>
> (Deuteronomy 7:9)

> *"I will not take my love from him,*
> *nor will I ever betray my faithfulness.*
> *I will not violate my covenant*
> *or alter what my lips have uttered."*   (Psalm 89:33–34)

> *... the knowledge of the truth that leads to godliness – a faith and knowledge resting on the hope of eternal life, which God, who does not lie, promised before the beginning of time.*
>
> (Titus 1:1–2)

Oath – the confirmation of covenant

When a promise is confirmed by an oath it is given even greater seriousness or solemnity. This is because the person making the oath is calling on God to bear witness to the words, and is therefore answerable to God for the truth of the statement or the binding character of the promise. In other words, by using an oath the person is asking God to hold him accountable.

What is more, the person is acknowledging that his honor and credibility are at stake. That is, his reputation for worthy and principled behavior is dependent upon him keeping his sworn word.

An oath was considered so serious in ancient times that if it was taken, it put the person's promise beyond question, and his word beyond the possibility of doubt. Even today if a person gives false evidence under oath before a court or tribunal, he or she is guilty of the serious crime of perjury.

> *People swear by someone greater than themselves, and the oath confirms what is said and puts an end to all argument.*
>   (Hebrews 6:16)

Thus in Israel, if a person entrusted an animal to his neighbor for safe keeping and it died, was injured or strayed, the issue was settled if the neighbor took an oath before the Lord that he did not lay hands on the other person's property. The owner was bound to accept this oath and no restitution was required (Exodus 22:11).

God's covenants are always based on his promises and confirmed by an oath.

> *But God will surely come to your aid and take you up out of this land to the land he promised on oath to Abraham, Isaac and Jacob.*   (Genesis 50:24)

> *You are standing here in order to enter into a covenant with the* Lord *your God, a covenant the* Lord *is making with you this day and sealing with an oath, to confirm to you this day as his people, that he may be your God as he promised you and as he swore to your fathers, Abraham, Isaac and Jacob.*
>   (Deuteronomy 29:12–13)

> *And it was not without an oath! Others became priests without any oath, but he became a priest with an oath when God said to him: "The Lord has sworn and will not change his mind: 'You are a priest for ever.'"* *Because of this oath, Jesus has become the guarantee of a better covenant.*   (Hebrews 7:20–22)

God's oath, however, is not an appeal to a higher authority than himself. It could only be an appeal to his own holy character.

God can swear by nothing higher than his own holiness, because holiness is nothing less than the essential uniqueness of God. There is no one holy but God (1 Samuel 2:2), thus holiness is God's "God-ness." God by his oath is putting his character, his holiness, his very God-ness at stake as a guarantee of his faithfulness to his promises.

> *"Once for all, I have sworn by my holiness –*
>   *and I will not lie to David –*
> *that his line will continue for ever*
>   *and his throne endure before me like the sun."*
>   (Psalm 89:35–36)

> *When God made his promise to Abraham, since there was no one greater for him to swear by, he swore by himself, saying, "I will surely bless you and give you many descendents."*
>   (Hebrews 6:13–14)

> *Because God wanted to make the unchanging nature of his purpose very clear to the heirs of what was promised, he confirmed it with an oath. God did this so that, by two unchangeable things in which it is impossible for God to lie, we who have fled to take hold of the hope offered to us may be greatly encouraged.*   (Hebrews 6:17–18)

Sacrifice – the sealing of covenant

The third act in establishing covenant is probably the most solemn and striking of all. The only way covenant is entered into is by sacrifice, and sacrifice means the shedding of blood.

> *When Moses had proclaimed every commandment of the law to all the people, he took the blood of calves, together with water, scarlet wool and branches of hyssop, and sprinkled the scroll and all the people. He said, "This is the blood of the covenant, which God has commanded you to keep."*   (Hebrews 9:19–20)

There are several important issues involved in the sacrifice:

Atonement

Firstly, in the covenants between God and people, the restoration of a relationship is possible only if the question of sin is satisfactorily dealt with. Thus covenant and forgiveness go hand in hand.

For example, the promise of the new covenant in Jeremiah 31:31–34 begins with the declaration, *"The time is coming when I will make a new covenant with the house of Israel"* and ends with the assurance, *"I will forgive their wickedness and will remember their sins no more."*

The new covenant passage in Ezekiel 36:25–28 begins with the promise, *"I will cleanse you from all your impurities and from all your idols"* and ends with the covenant formula, *"You will be my people and I will be your God."*

But forgiveness is possible only through atonement, and atonement is possible only through sacrifice. And sacrifice means the shedding of blood, *"for without the shedding of blood there is no forgiveness"* (Hebrews 9:22).

Atonement is the covering of sin by something that robs it of its power to separate human beings and God. That something is the blood of Christ.

> Then he took the cup, gave thanks and offered it to them, saying, *"Drink from it, all of you. This is my blood of the covenant, which is poured out for many for the forgiveness of sins."*
>
> (Matthew 26:27–28)

Separation

Secondly, when people entered a covenant, the sacrificial ritual was known as "cutting" the covenant. The sacrifice was cut in two pieces and the parties to the covenant walked between its pieces.

About God's covenant with Abraham we read,

> So the Lord said to him, *"Bring me a heifer, a goat and a ram, each three years old, along with a dove and a young pigeon. Abram brought all these to him, cut them in two and arranged the halves opposite each other; the birds, however, he did not cut in half ... When the sun had set and darkness had fallen, a smoking firepot with a blazing torch appeared and passed

between the pieces. On that day the Lord *made a covenant with Abram ... "* (Genesis 15:9–10, 17–18)

Here, not only Abraham, but also God himself, passed between the pieces and made the covenant.

What is symbolized here is the parties to the covenant acknowledging their own deaths. They have entered covenant by death and the sacrifice represents their death. That is why the Bible makes no distinction between the Greek words for covenant and testament or will.

In the case of a will [covenant], *it is necessary to prove the death of the one who made it, because a will is in force only when somebody has died; it never takes effect while the one who made it is living.* (Hebrews 9:16–17)

That death means final and irrevocable separation from their previous life. They have given up their right to live any longer for themselves. They acknowledge that they have died to those rights and henceforth they live for, and if need be will die for the other party to the covenant. Whatever the covenant partner needs, they will supply. Whatever the covenant partner asks for, they will freely give.

In Genesis 18, Abraham asked God to spare Sodom if there were 50 righteous people in the city, and because of the covenant relationship (see verses 17–19) God said "Yes." Abraham said, "for 45?" "for 40?" "for 30, 20, 10?" and God said "Yes" every time. In the end it was Abraham who stopped asking. God never said "No" or refused his requests.

In Genesis 22, it is God who asked something of Abraham. He asked for Isaac, Abraham's only son, to be offered up as a burnt offering. Abraham never hesitated, because he too knew covenant rights and covenant obligations.

Hebrews 11:17–19 tells us that Abraham believed that he would have to sacrifice Isaac and cremate his body (remember, it was a burnt offering), but because God would never break his promise, he would have to raise Isaac back to life from the ashes! No wonder Abraham is called the father of all those who have faith.

Curse on covenant breaking

Finally, the covenant has both blessings and curses. The sacrifice signifies that the parties symbolically call down upon themselves the curse of dismemberment if they break the covenant. When God cut the covenant with Abraham and passed between the pieces of the sacrifice, he said in effect, "May I cease to be God if I ever break my covenant with Abraham."

In Jeremiah 34, God says to those who have profaned his name and broken covenant:

> *Those who have violated my covenant and have not fulfilled the terms of the covenant they made before me, I will treat like the calf they cut in two and then walked between its pieces. The leaders of Judah and Jerusalem, the court officials, the priests and all the people of the land who walked between the pieces of the calf, I will hand over their enemies who seek their lives. Their dead bodies will become food for the birds of the air and the beasts of the earth.* (Jeremiah 34:18–20)

This is the curse on covenant breaking coming into operation.

3

The Abrahamic covenant

We come now to examine the covenants between God and human beings. If covenant is a bonded relationship between God and people, we have still to ask:

▶ What is the nature and scope of that relationship?

▶ What has God bound himself by promise and oath to do or to give?

▶ What are we bound to do so as to keep the covenant and receive its benefits?

To answer these questions, we will examine the four most important covenants of scripture,

1. The covenant with Abraham

2. The covenant with Israel (the Mosaic covenant)

3. The covenant with David, and

4. The new covenant of Jesus Christ.

The covenant and faith

We have seen that covenant is always God's gracious initiative towards human beings, and the Abrahamic covenant is no exception. *"God in his grace gave it to Abraham through a promise"* (Galatians 3:18). But because the covenant is of grace, the human response must be of faith. It is of critical importance to understand why this is so.

21

■ **Grace and faith always go together.** It is significant that when Paul addresses this topic in his letter to the Romans, he bases his argument on the Abrahamic covenant.

> *Therefore, the promise comes by faith, so that it may be by grace and may be guaranteed to all Abraham's offspring – not only to those who are of the law but also to those who are of the faith of Abraham. He is the father of us all. As it is written: "I have made you a father of many nations."* (Romans 4:16)

Grace, in other words, can never be earned. It can only be received by faith, that is, by trusting it as a free gift.

> *What does the scripture say? "Abraham believed God, and it was credited to him as righteousness." Now to one who works, wages are not credited as a gift, but as an obligation. However, to the one who does not work but trusts God who justifies the wicked, that person's faith is credited as righteousness.*
> (Romans 4:3–5)

■ **Faith is much more than mere intellectual assent to an idea or concept.** Faith has its source and its object in the character of the personal God who has bound himself by covenant. For Abraham it meant that he had to renounce all his human efforts to secure the promise. He had to trust solely in the God of the covenant to work in the present and the future to accomplish what he said he would do.

What was true of Abraham was also true of all the men and women of the old covenant. Moses, Joshua, Gideon, Samuel, David, and countless others, as Hebrews 11 makes quite clear. *"All these people were still living in faith when they died"* (Hebrews 11:13).

Faith is therefore also the key to the new covenant, and this again is linked back to the Abrahamic covenant. *"So those who have faith are blessed along with Abraham, the man of faith"* (Galatians 3:9).

The promise

The covenants of scripture have an essential unity, in that they express a progressive and expanding revelation of God's plan of blessing for the human race. This plan of God is known in scripture as *"the promise."* Peter referred to it on the day of Pentecost when he said,

> *The promise is for you and your children and for all who are far off – for all whom the Lord our God will call.*   (Acts 2:39)

The promise is the plan of God in human history to bring a universal blessing to the whole world, through the agency of a divinely chosen human offspring.

Introduction to the promise
Immediately after the Fall, human sin was met not only with the necessary judgment, but also with God's word of grace. This was the promise of the woman's seed (offspring), and from it a male individual who would crush the serpent's head.

God cursed the serpent, adding:

> *And I will put enmity*
>   *between you and the woman,*
>   *and between your offspring and hers;*
> *he will crush your head,*
>   *and you will strike his heel.*   (Genesis 3:15)

After the flood, there was a second grace word of God, the blessing of Shem, *"May God extend the territory of Japheth; may Japheth live in the tents of Shem"* (Genesis 9:27). In other words, the promise was to be realized through the Semitic people.

The call of Abraham
But after Babel there was something new, a succession of individuals, beginning with Abraham, called by God as his appointed means of fulfilling the word of blessing to all humankind.

Even before the covenant was entered into, the language of blessing was very evident in Abraham's call:

> *"I will make you into a great nation*
>   *and I will bless you;*

> *I will make your name great,*
>   *and you will be a blessing.*
> *I will bless those who bless you,*
>   *and whoever curses you I will curse;*
> *and all peoples on earth*
>   *will be blessed through you."*   (Genesis 12:2–3)

The provisions of the covenant with Abraham

The covenant with Abraham was God's solemn promise to him (Romans 4:13), confirmed by an oath (Genesis 50:24) and entered into through sacrifice (Genesis 15:8–21). Its content was very specific.

> *Abram fell face down, and God said to him, "As for me, this is my covenant with you: You will be the father of many nations. No longer will you be called Abram; your name will be Abraham, for I have made you a father of many nations. I will make you very fruitful; I will make nations of you, and kings will come from you. I will establish my covenant as an everlasting covenant between me and you and your descendents after you for the generations to come, to be your God and the God of your descendents after you. The whole land of Canaan, where you are now an alien, I will give as an everlasting possession to you and your descendents after you; and I will be their God."*
>   (Genesis 17:3–8)

The content of the promise to Abraham was basically three-fold: a seed, a land, and a universal blessing. Each is highly significant.

1. The seed

The ancient promise to Eve was revived. Childless Abraham was promised offspring, or a *"seed"* who would inherit the land of Canaan. They would be as numerous as the stars, would possess the cities of their enemies, and would be the means through whom all nations on earth would be blessed (Genesis 12:7; 13:15–16; 15:5; 18–20; 17:7–9; 19; 21:12; 22:17–18).

Throughout scripture, the seed has both a collective and an individual reference. Sometimes, it refers to one person; at other times to the many descendents of the family.

■ **In its collective sense**, the promised seed is inseparably linked to the Israelite race and the promise of land, but it is not limited to that fulfillment, as Paul points out:

> *Understand, then, that those who believe are children of Abraham ... If you belong to Christ, then you are Abraham's seed, and heirs according to the promise.* (Galatians 3:7, 29)

■ **In its individual sense**, it has reference to successive sons of the patriarchs. In each case, the firstborn of the flesh was set aside in favor of the firstborn of promise. Ishmael was set aside in favor of Isaac (Genesis 17:19–21; Galatians 4:22–31), Esau was set aside in favor of Jacob (Genesis 28:12–14) and Simeon was set aside in favor of Judah (Genesis 49:10).

■ **But its ultimate fulfillment** is in the person of Jesus Christ, the promised seed who would crush the serpent's head, and the seed of Abraham through whom all families on earth have been blessed.

> *The promises were spoken to Abraham and to his seed. The scripture does not say "and to seeds," meaning many people, but "and to your seed," meaning one person, who is Christ.* (Galatians 3:16)

2. A land

In the Abrahamic covenant, the promise of the seed is inseparable from the promise of the land. We need to understand why this is so.

■ **From the beginning, human beings have been given a special relationship with the earth**. Adam was placed in the garden to work it and to take care of it. When human beings fell, the whole creation was disordered by their sin; the earth is cursed because of it (Genesis 3:17).

■ **God's grace is extended not only towards human beings but towards creation**. The restoration of covenant relationship, or human redemption, can therefore be understood only as an integral part of the redemption of all creation. Not only are the covenant people chosen, the land is chosen as well:

> *It is a land the* Lord *your God cares for; the eyes of the* Lord *your God are continually on it from the beginning of the year to its end.*   (Deuteronomy 11:12)

The fulfillment of the land promise began with the partial occupation and conquest of Canaan under Joshua. A greater and more complete specific, geographic and national fulfillment still lies in the future.

At the same time, just as the seed of Abraham is ultimately extended to include those who believe in Christ, so too the land promise also expands.

> *Abraham and his offspring received the promise that he would be heir of the world.*   (Romans 4:13)

The land of Canaan, we discover, turns out to be but a staging post on the way to world dominion, that is, the kingdom of God. But just as world dominion of the seed of Abraham will be literally fulfilled, so must the national dominion of Israel be literally fulfilled.

3. The universal blessing

The spiritual and material blessings that God bestowed on Abraham were not only because he was *"the friend of God."* They were in order that he might be a blessing, and so that all peoples on earth would be blessed through him (Genesis 12:2–3) and through his offspring (Genesis 22:18).

In the lives of Abraham's descendents we find that:

- **The emphasis in the life of Isaac, the child of promise, was on the seed**, and Abraham's fleshly attempts to fulfill the promise.

- **The emphasis in the life of Jacob was on the land**, and on his fleshly attempts to obtain it by cheating Esau of his rights as the firstborn.

- **The emphasis in the life of Joseph, as the savior of Egypt, was on the beginning of the blessing to the nations.**

The ultimate fulfillment of the universal blessing, however, is the justification of the Gentiles by faith and the gift of the Holy Spirit.

The Scripture foresaw that God would justify the Gentiles by faith, and announced the gospel in advance to Abraham: "All nations will be blessed through you." So those who have faith are blessed along with Abraham, the man of faith.

He [Christ] redeemed us in order that the blessing given to Abraham might come to the Gentiles through Christ Jesus, so that by faith we might receive the promise of the Spirit.

(Galatians 3:8–9, 14)

Nature of the Abrahamic covenant

Finally, note the following important points about the Abrahamic covenant:

■ **It is an everlasting covenant** (Genesis 17:7, 13, 19), therefore, it has remained in force ever since it was made with Abraham. Moses pleaded the Abrahamic covenant when God threatened to destroy Israel because of their sin (Exodus 32:13). Because of the covenant with Abraham, God repeatedly intervened in Israel's crises (Exodus 2:24; 2 Kings 13:23; Psalm 105:8–11).

Zechariah's prophecy at the birth of John the Baptist declared that God had remembered his covenant with Abraham (Luke 1:72–73), and Paul says in Galatians 3:14 that the work of redemption was in order to bring the Gentiles into its blessing.

■ **It is a three-party covenant**, that is, it was made by God with Abraham and with Abraham's descendents. In a three-party covenant, even if one party breaks the covenant, the other two parties remain bound.

Thus the unbelieving seed of Abraham cannot break God's covenant with Abraham; they themselves will lose the covenant promises, but the promises still stand for future generations to enter into if they meet the covenant requirements of faith and obedience (Hebrews 3:16–4:3).

■ **It is all-embracing**. God became their God, therefore, the covenant embraced the entirety of the lives of the patriarchs and the totality of their relationship with God.

Thus it included:

- **Spiritual blessings.** God would be the God of Abraham and his descendents after him. He would make Abraham's name great and would bless those who blessed him and curse whoever cursed him (Genesis 12:3; 17:7).

- **Material blessings**, including great wealth and the land of Canaan as an everlasting possession (Genesis 13:2; 15:8).

- **A new status or standing**, and therefore new, God-given names. Abram became Abraham, Isaac was named by God and Jacob became Israel (Genesis 17:5, 19; 32:28). Henceforth, God calls himself the God of Abraham, Isaac and Israel (1 Kings 18:36; 1 Chronicles 29:18).

4

The Mosaic covenant

In the four centuries between Joseph and Moses, there had already been a partial fulfillment of the promise to Abraham of numerous offspring. The family had become a nation of over 2 million, but they had also become a slave people. In this situation, the covenant with Abraham is declared to be the grounds for God's intervention on their behalf.

> *"Moreover, I have heard the groaning of the Israelites, whom the Egyptians are enslaving, and I have remembered my covenant."*
> (Exodus 6:5)

God's remembering his covenant does not have to do with mere recall. It is God allowing his covenant commitment to affect his actions.

With this there is also God's revelation of his name as Yahweh.

> *"I am the LORD [Yahweh]. I appeared to Abraham, to Isaac and to Jacob as God Almighty [El Shaddai], but my name the LORD I did not make known to them."* (Exodus 6:2–3)

Yahweh is a salvation name, the most frequently used name of God in the Old Testament. The name itself had been known to the patriarchs, but God would now reveal the significance of that name by his acts of salvation on behalf of his people.

The covenant at Sinai

After Israel's experience of deliverance from Egypt and the crossing of the Red Sea, they journeyed to Mount Sinai where Moses received the law and the pattern for the Tabernacle. This was God giving the covenant to Israel.

> *Then the* LORD *said to Moses, "Write down these words, for in accordance with these words I have made a covenant with you and with Israel." Moses was there with the* LORD *forty days and forty nights without eating bread or drinking water. And he wrote on the tablets the words of the covenant – the Ten Command-ments.* (Exodus 34:27–28)

▶ ***The Mosaic covenant, that is, the covenant with Israel is an expansion and application of the Abrahamic covenant – the promise made to a chosen family is now extended to a chosen nation.***

Let us see what was involved in this expansion of the promise.

1. The seed

The Abrahamic promise of the seed is now developed in two ways.

(a) Israel is God's son, his firstborn (Exodus 4:22–23)

"Son" and "Firstborn" are henceforth collective terms for Israel (Jeremiah 31:9), but are also terms referring to the specific individual, the Messiah, who would ultimately come to fulfill the words of the promise.

> *When Israel was a child, I loved him,*
> *and out of Egypt I called my son.*
> (Hosea 11:1; cf. Matthew 2:15)

(b) Israel is the people of God (Exodus 5:1; 7:14)

■ **They are a nation**, that is, they are now sufficiently numer-ous and unified to become an ethnic social group with its own distinctive culture, norms and outlook. Besides this they are bound to God in a special way by his sovereign choice.

■ **They are God's inheritance and his treasured possession** (Deuteronomy 9:29; Psalm 33:12), literally, *"God's special, moveable treasure."*

2. The land

The theme of the land is a major one in Israel's history. For example, salvation is described as bringing Israel out of the land of Egypt and into the land of promise (Exodus 3:8).

Note the following important points:

■ **The land is a gift**, and comes from God's love for his people (Exodus 6:8; Deuteronomy 1:7–8; 6:10). But although the land is given, Israel still had to possess it. They could not take it by their own power, as they found to their cost in the Kadesh (Numbers 14:39–45).

■ **The land always belongs to God**, therefore, it could not be alienated from the tribe (Numbers 36:9); and even if it is sold, it must in the year of Jubilee be returned to the original owner (Leviticus 25:23–28).

■ **The land symbolized blessing**. It was a *"good and spacious land, a land flowing with milk and honey"* (Exodus 3:8). Therefore, land is also associated with "rest" (Deuteronomy 12:9–10), that is, a particular quality of life that consisted of:

• Victory over all their enemies,

• The cessation of internal strife, and

• The fulfillment of all God's promises (Joshua 21:43–45).

■ **Occupancy of the land necessitated a certain lifestyle.** Because God dwelt among his people and had placed his Name there (Deuteronomy 12:5), sin had the effect of polluting or defiling the land (Numbers 35:33; Jeremiah 3:2). Rebellion or unfaithfulness could mean that occupancy of the land was lost (Deuteronomy 28:36–37; 64–65).

3. The universal blessing

The role that God had in store for Israel was the most exalted imaginable.

▶ *God had chosen to dwell among them.*

As well as the general or structural presence of God in all creation (Psalm 139:7–12; Jeremiah 23:23–24), Israel experienced greater intensifications of God's presence, expressing his desire for intimacy with his people:

- **God's accompanying presence in the wilderness**, manifested in the cloud and the fire (Exodus 13:20–22; 16:10; 24:15–18), the presence, the glory, and the Name.

- **God's tabernacle presence**. The central aspect of the tabernacle is God's presence in the Ark of the Testimony and the Mercy Seat (Exodus 25:10–22).

- **God's theophanic presence**. These were highly intense, sharply focused moments of divine appearance, commonly face-to-face encounters at watershed times in the lives of individuals or communities (Exodus 33:11; 34:29–35; Joshua 5:13–15).

Israel was to be a kingdom of priests, that is, relating to God as subjects of their King (Deuteronomy 33:5), and to the nations as royal priests. In other words, they were to be mediators of God's grace to the ends of the earth.

As the record shows, Israel declined this privilege (Exodus 19:16–25; 20:18–21). The tribe of Levi received the priesthood and this purpose of God was delayed until the new covenant, when the church stepped into its priestly role (1 Peter 2:9).

The covenant and obedience

We have already seen that because covenant is always grace on

God's part, the necessary response on our part is always faith. Here is another corollary:

▶ **Because the terms of the covenant are always set by God, the necessary response on our part is always obedience.**

> *"Now if you obey me fully and keep my covenant, then out of all nations you will be my treasured possession. Although the whole earth is mine, you will be for me a kingdom of priests and a holy nation."* (Exodus 19:5–6)

Obedience is therefore the same as "keeping the covenant" (Deuteronomy 29:9; Leviticus 26:15, 44; 1 Kings 11:11; Psalm 78:10; 132:12; Isaiah 56:4; Jeremiah 11:6). So **disobedience is "violating the covenant"** (2 Kings 18:12; Jeremiah 34:17–18; Deuteronomy 17:2–3).

Therefore, just as we may say that from the human side there is no participation in covenant without faith, we may also say that there is equally no participation in covenant without obedience.

Nevertheless, although keeping the covenant involves obedience to its terms and conditions, it is important to understand that the terms and conditions do not make the covenant. In this a covenant differs radically from a contract.

A contract is formed by the terms and conditions to which the parties have agreed. Agreement to the terms creates the contract.

By contrast, **a covenant is formed by the bond of personal loyalty** into which the parties enter. The terms and conditions arise out of that bond; they do not create the bond, but they explain what that particular bonded relationship entails for both parties.

The Greek word for covenant or testament is *diatheke*, which means "to set something out in order." The covenant has this sense of orderliness and rightness. It sets forth terms and conditions, because God does not act out of caprice or whim.

For Israel the law was the *"Book of the Covenant"* (Exodus 24:7). It did not create the covenant relationship between God and Israel, but it articulated in detail how this was to be understood and what was involved in maintaining fellowship with God. In other words, Israel was in covenant with God by grace, but the law explained what it then meant for Israel that God was their God and they were his people.

In the same way, for us, the entire New Testament is the book of the new covenant of our Lord and Savior Jesus Christ. In it, God makes his covenant will and purposes known to us so that we are not left guessing as to what they might be, or what is required of us to live in covenant relationship with him. We will come back to this in more detail when we deal with the new covenant.

The law and holiness to the Lord

One of the startling features of the covenant with Israel is its emphasis on holiness. To Israel first, God revealed his holiness. Over 40% of the appearances of the word holy in the Old Testament are found in Exodus, Leviticus, Numbers and Deuteronomy. Because Israel belongs to God, holiness is not an optional extra, but an essential feature of life.

> *The LORD said to Moses, "Speak to the entire assembly of Israel and say to them: 'Be holy because I, the LORD your God, am holy.'"*   (Leviticus 19:1–2)

The law of God is given to show Israel what it means to be holy. This is because Israel is not serving an arbitrary deity, but One who makes his will known and is consistent in all his dealings. Israel was given:

- **The moral law**, in the Ten Commandments (Exodus 20:1–17; Deuteronomy 5:6–21) summarizing God's moral boundary rules for human life.

- **The civil law**, the application of the moral law to public life.

- **The ceremonial law**, the sacrificial system to deal with sin and failure.

The law leading to Christ

The law had, however, another essential function that only it could fulfill, as Paul explains:

So the law was put in charge to lead us to Christ that we might be justified by faith.   (Galatians 3:24)

The New American Standard Bible puts it as *"the law has become our tutor."* The way in which it fulfilled this function can be summarized briefly as follows:

- **By revealing the holiness of God** and the requirements of his holiness, it showed us our sin (Romans 7:7–13).

- **By revealing the root of our sin as within us** – the set of inner values known as *"the flesh"* – it showed our total incapacity to live by external law, even when that law is written by the finger of God (Romans 7:14–25; 8:7; Galatians 5:19–21).

- **By showing that the only possible means of justification is by faith in Jesus Christ** (Galatians 3:23–24).

We will deal with the implications of all this more fully when we come to the new covenant.

5

The Davidic covenant

The covenant made by God with David is recorded in 2 Samuel 7:10–17 and 1 Chronicles 17:11–14. Although the word "covenant" does not appear in either of these passages, God's promises on that occasion are described in Psalm 89 as God's covenant with David.

> *He will call out to me, "You are my Father,*
> *my God, the Rock my Savior."*
> *I will also appoint him my firstborn,*
> *the most exalted of the kings of the earth.*
> *I will maintain my love to him for ever,*
> *and my covenant with him will never fail.*
> *I will establish his line for ever,*
> *his throne as long as the heavens endure.*
> *. . . I will not take my love from him,*
> *nor will I ever betray my faithfulness.*
> *I will not violate my covenant*
> *or alter what my lips have uttered.*
> *Once for all, I have sworn by my holiness –*
> *and I will not lie to David –*
> *that his line will continue for ever*
> *and his throne endure before me like the sun;*
> *it will be established for ever like the moon,*
> *the faithful witness in the sky.*   (Psalm 89:26–29, 33–35)

Like the covenant with Abraham, that with David is everlasting. It is called the *"holy and sure blessings promised to David"* (Acts 13:34) or God's *"faithful love promised to David"* (Isaiah 55:3).

David's last words affirm that confidence:

> *Has he not made with me an everlasting covenant,*
> *arranged and secured in every part?* (2 Samuel 23:5)

We now have to see just what these covenant promises contained, and why this has enduring significance, ranking with the Abrahamic covenant and surpassed only by the new covenant of Jesus Christ. The promises to David centered on several distinctive features.

A royal dynasty

David had proposed building a temple, a house for God, but this was not to be: the task was reserved for David's son, Solomon. But God declared to David that *"the LORD himself will establish a house for you"* (2 Samuel 7:11). This *"house"* was not a residence, because David had already built himself a palace. It could only refer to his household, that is, his family and descendents.

Everywhere we go in the Old Testament, we come across the "father's house" (Genesis 12:1; 24:7; 2 Samuel 2:8 etc.). It is the strong, enduring community of the family (2 Samuel 9:1–3).

David replied,

> *Who am I, O Sovereign LORD, and what is my family, that you have brought me this far? And as if this were not enough in your sight, O Sovereign LORD, you have also spoken about the future of the house of your servant.* (2 Samuel 7:18–19)

This was a new addition to the promise. It meant that **all that had been offered to the patriarchs and Israel in the previous covenants was now being offered to David's dynasty**, in other words, a succession of rulers from his family.

An everlasting kingdom

One item in the promise to Abraham was that *"kings will come from you"* (Genesis 17:6, 16; 35:11) and in the covenant with Israel God said that there would be a kingdom (Exodus 19:6;

Numbers 24:7). Now that kingdom was assigned in perpetuity
to David and his descendents.

> *Your house and your kingdom shall endure for ever before me;*
> *your throne shall be established for ever.*   (2 Samuel 7:16)

> *For this is what the* LORD *says, "David will never fail to have a*
> *man to sit on the throne of the house of Israel . . . If you can break*
> *my covenant with the day and my covenant with the night, so*
> *that day and night no longer come at my appointed time, then*
> *my covenant with David my servant . . . can be broken and David*
> *will no longer have a descendent to reign on his throne."*
>   (Jeremiah 33:17, 20–21)

When David realized the magnitude of what had been given to
him, he was completely overwhelmed.

> *Who am I, O Sovereign* LORD, *and what is my family, that you*
> *have brought me thus far? And as if this were not enough in your*
> *sight, O Sovereign* LORD, *you have also spoken about the future of*
> *your servant. Is this your usual way of dealing with people, O*
> *Sovereign* LORD?   (2 Samuel 7:18–19)

An alternative translation of the last phrase is, *"This is the charter*
for humanity." In other words, the ancient promise of God to
Abraham regarding a universal blessing would continue, only
now it would involve a king and a kingdom. This kingdom and
its blessing would bring within its scope the future of all
mankind.

The ark, the city and the kingdom

The presence and the power of God in Israel are intimately
connected with the ark of the covenant. Therefore, David
brought the ark into the tent in Jerusalem, David's tabernacle,
until he could build a temple. He established the kingdom given
to him by God (2 Samuel 6:1–19).

> *For the* LORD *has chosen Zion,*
>   *he has desired it for his dwelling:*

> *"This is my resting place for ever and ever;*
>   *here I will sit enthroned, for I have desired it."*
>   (Psalm 132:13–14)

This is the beginning of the insight that absorbed the attention of the prophets – the coming of the kingdom of God and the Messiah, the Son of David, who would reign over the whole earth.

> *"But you, Bethlehem Ephrathah,*
>   *though you are small among the clans of Judah,*
> *out of you will come for me*
>   *one who will be ruler over Israel,*
> *whose origins are from of old,*
>   *from ancient times."*   (Micah 5:2)

Even when the Davidic house or dynasty was in tatters, now merely a hut or tent, it would rise from the ashes under a new, coming "David," and would extend its authority to the Gentile nations.

> *"After this I will return and rebuild David's fallen tent. Its ruins I will rebuild, and I will restore it, that the remnant of humanity may seek the Lord, and all the Gentiles who bear my name,"* *says the Lord, who does these things.*   (Acts 15:16–17)

James here is taking the prophecy of Amos 9:11–12 regarding the restoration of David's tent, and applying it to the preaching of the Gospel to the Gentiles.

A Messianic king – the Son of God

The future Davidic king is addressed as God in Psalm 45, and the writer of Hebrews applies verses 6–7 to Christ, the Son of God:

> *Your throne, O God, will last for ever and ever;*
>   *and righteousness will be the scepter of your kingdom.*
> *You have loved righteousness and hated wickedness;*
>   *therefore God, your God, has set you above your companions*
>   *by anointing you with the oil of joy.*   (Hebrews 1:8–9)

> *For to us a child is born,*
> *to us a son is given,*
> *and the government will be on his shoulders.*
> *And he will be called*
> *Wonderful Counselor, Mighty God,*
> *Everlasting Father, Prince of Peace.*
> *Of the increase of his government and peace*
> *there will be no end.*
> *He will reign on David's throne*
> *and over his kingdom,*
> *establishing and upholding it*
> *with justice and righteousness*
> *from that time on and for ever.*   (Isaiah 9:6–7)

■ **The fulfillment of the covenant with David came with the birth of Jesus Christ**, as the angel Gabriel made very clear to the virgin Mary.

> *"You will be with child and give birth to a son, and you are to give him the name Jesus. He will be great and will be called the Son of the Most High. The Lord God will give him the throne of his father David, and he will reign over the house of Jacob for ever; his kingdom will never end ... So the holy one to be born will be called the Son of God."*   (Luke 1:31–33, 35)

Fifteen times in the Gospels, Jesus is referred to as the Son of David. In Matthew 1:1 he is *"Jesus Christ, the son of David, the son of Abraham,"* establishing his identity as the Abrahamic-Davidic Messiah and legal heir to David's throne.

In Revelation 5:5, he is the *"Lion of the tribe of Judah, the Root of David,"* and in Revelation 22:16 *"the Root and the Offspring of David, and the bright Morning Star."* He holds the *"key of David"* (Revelation 3:7), that is, the authority of the Davidic kingdom, which translates into the authority to prevail against the kingdom of Satan (Luke 10:18–19).

Christ came as the Messiah, the anointed King, to bring the kingdom of God to earth. He will come a second time to consummate that kingdom – the rock cut out without human hands, that becomes a huge mountain and fills the whole earth (Daniel 2:34–35; 44–45).

6

The new covenant

In the history of God's redemptive covenants with human beings, there remained certain critical issues. These stood in the way of God achieving his desire for an everlasting relationship of personal intimacy with people, even after the covenant with David.

One was *the need for a final solution to the sin problem.* The sacrificial system spoke in faith of sin being covered, but the blood of animals could not deal with the question of guilt nor could it clear the conscience of the worshiper (Hebrews 9:9).

The law of God, holy and righteous and good as it was (Romans 7:12) was external to people. It could show us what we ought to do, but could not enable us to do it because of the internalized sinful values of our fallen nature (Romans 8:3). All God's dealings with Israel proved over and over again that when external law and inner values disagree, in the long run inner values will win out every time.

People not only lack the power to obey the law of God, we lack the motivation to even desire to obey it. Our natural mindset is hostile to God, and does not submit to his law, nor can it do so (Romans 8:7). Furthermore, the entirety of human nature is affected by sin and rebellion so that there is no place where we can stand to get the leverage to change our attitude to God (Romans 1:9–32).

In this situation, *there is an enormous gulf between human beings and God.* People are literally lost and can never find their way back to God, even if they should try. Any initiative must therefore come from God. We are limited to God's grace for salvation.

*There is no difference, for all have sinned and fall short of
the glory of God, and are justified freely by his grace through the
redemption that came by Christ Jesus.* 　　　(Romans 3:23–24)

Prophecies of the new covenant

It is in this context that the prophets began to speak about a
new covenant – not new in the sense that it totally replaced
what had gone before, but in representing a dramatic break-
through to finally achieve the purpose of the covenants.

Two of the key passages for understanding this radically new
covenant are in Jeremiah and Ezekiel, parts of which we have
already looked at.

"The time is coming," declares the Lord,
　"when I will make a new covenant
with the house of Israel
　and with the house of Judah.
It will not be like the covenant
　I made with their ancestors
when I took them by the hand
　to lead them out of Egypt,
because they broke my covenant,
　though I was a husband to them,"

declares the Lord.

"This is the covenant that I will make with
　　the house of Israel
after that time," declares the Lord.
"I will put my law in their minds
　and write it on their hearts.
I will be their God,
　and they will be my people.
No longer will they teach their neighbors,
　or say to one another, 'Know the Lord*',*
because they will all know me,
　from the least of them to the greatest,"

declares the Lord.

"For I will forgive their wickedness
　and will remember their sins no more."

(Jeremiah 31:31–34)

"I will sprinkle clean water on you, and you will be clean; I will cleanse you from all your impurities and from all your idols. I will give you a new heart and put a new spirit in you; I will remove from you your heart of stone and give you a heart of flesh. And I will put my Spirit in you and move you to follow my decrees and be careful to keep my laws. You will live in the land I gave your ancestors; you will be my people, and I will be your God." (Ezekiel 36:25–28)

There is a close link between the concepts of *shalom* (peace) and *b'riyth* (covenant). *Shalom* is the state of those united in full harmony of the soul with each other, and *b'riyth* is the bonded relationship with all the privileges and duties implied in it.

Both words may be used together. For example, a covenant is a covenant of peace (Ezekiel 34:25; Isaiah 54:10), or conversely to enter into covenant is to *"make peace"* (Joshua 10:1, 4; 2 Samuel 10:19; 1 Kings 22:44).

The new covenant, accomplished by the life, death and resurrection of Jesus Christ, is also described as *"making peace."*

For God was pleased to have all his fullness dwell in him, and through him to reconcile to himself all things, whether things on earth or things in heaven, by making peace through his blood, shed on the cross. (Colossians 1:19–20)

We now turn to examine the way in which the new covenant achieves the covenant goal of God's heart.

The final solution to the problem of sin

All sin is an offence against God's nature that God cannot overlook and must judge. God's wrath is his implacable enmity against sin (Romans 1:18). Furthermore, only judgment ends the destructive power of sin.

God, therefore, cannot forgive human beings until our sin is judged. We also must recognize God's perfect justice in judging and punishing sin and the rightness of his wrath against it.

If we are to escape judgment, we need a sin-bearer on our behalf, but only a sinless man could perfectly recognize the divine justice of God's wrath against sin and perfectly agree with it. Therefore, we need a sinless sin-bearer.

In Jesus Christ, God reaches across the divide between the infinite God and finite human beings, as well as across the moral divide between the holy God and sinful human beings. God becomes flesh (John 1:14) and the God-Man is willingly made sin for us:

> *God made him who had no sin to be sin for us, so that in him we might become the righteousness of God.*
>
> (2 Corinthians 5:21)

In the incarnation, Jesus became:

- Our substitute, a man for all people:

  > *For Christ died for sins once for all, the righteous for the unrighteous, to bring you to God.*   (1 Peter 3:18)

- Our representative, a man as all people:

  > *For Christ's love compels us, because we are convinced that one died for all, and therefore all died. And he died for all, that those who live should no longer live for themselves but for him who died for them and was raised again*
  >
  > (2 Corinthians 5:14–15)

On the cross, Christ bore God's judgment on sin and with a perfect human heart, agreed with God's justice. Therefore, divine judgment and wrath fell on the one and only place where it could become redemptive. The holiness of God's character and the holiness of God's law were upheld.

Now God can justly forgive individuals who by repentance and faith become identified with Christ's substitutionary and representative death on their behalf.

> *But if we walk in the light, as he is in the light, we have fellowship with one another, and the blood of Jesus, his Son, purifies us from all sin. If we claim to be without sin, we deceive ourselves and the truth is not in us. If we confess our sins, he is faithful and just and will forgive us our sins and purify us from all unrighteousness.*   (1 John 1:7–9)

Forgiveness deals with the guilt of sin, while purification or cleansing deals with the stain. The problem of sin has been dealt with, but the problem of obedience remains.

The internalized law

In Jeremiah 31:33, God says that the first step in a complete solution to the problem of covenant obedience is to internalize the law. This time it would be written not on stone tablets, but on human hearts. It is to become an internal law, not an external one. Instead of being a standard to keep or even a principle to live by, the law of God is to become our internal motivation. Instead of knowing what we should do but lacking the motivation to do it, we will be moved from within to freely keep God's law (Ezekiel 36:27).

But how is this internalizing of the law to be accomplished? It is only through the incarnation. The importance of the incarnation to our salvation cannot be emphasized enough.

> *For if, when we were God's enemies, we were reconciled to him through the death of his Son, how much more, having been reconciled, shall we be saved through his life!*
>
> (Romans 5:10)

Jesus is called by Paul, *"the last Adam"* (1 Corinthians 15:45). He came to create a new beginning for humankind. As the progenitor of the new covenant people, he had to fulfill in his human life the promises of the new covenant. His death solved the problem of guilt and forgiveness, but his life was the vehicle whereby the law of God was internalized.

How did he do it? By perfect, painstaking, persistent obedience in every situation and in every circumstance, in times of stress and times of boredom, over great issues and small issues, writing God's law on a human heart.

> *Therefore, when Christ came into the world, he said, "Sacrifice and offering you did not desire, but a body you prepared for me; with burnt offerings and sin offerings you were not pleased. Then I said, 'Here I am – it is written about me in the scroll – I have come to do your will, O God.'"*   (Hebrews 10:5–7)

In his incarnate life, Jesus created in himself, and for us, a new self that is *"created to be like God in true righteousness and holiness"* (Ephesians 4:24). And this is the nature that is born in us by the Holy Spirit.

Paul deals at length with the inner dynamics of the new covenant in his second letter to the Corinthians:

> *You show that you are a letter from Christ, the result of our ministry, written not with ink but with the Spirit of the living God, not on tablets of stone but on tablets of human hearts ... He has made us competent as ministers of the new covenant – not of the letter but of the Spirit; for the letter kills, but the Spirit gives life.*   (2 Corinthians 3:3, 6)

New inner values, a heart of flesh

Not only is the law to be internalized, but under the new covenant, something is also to happen to the polluted human heart.

Sin is to be cleansed from it and the hostile inner values of the sinful nature are to be rendered inoperative.

> *Those who belong to Christ Jesus have crucified the sinful nature with its passions and desires.*   (Galatians 5:24)

In its place there is to be implanted in the heart a new set of inner values. We know them as the fruit of the Spirit.

> *But the fruit of the Spirit is love, joy, peace, patience, kindness, goodness, faithfulness, gentleness and self control.*
>   (Galatians 5:22–23)

"Against such things there is no law," Paul goes on to say, or to put it another way, "The law of God is not against such things." On the contrary, these inner values are in perfect harmony and concord with the internalized law. The problem of obedience is overcome! Right behavior becomes the natural correspondence of inner values and internalized law.

In the life of Jesus, the result of this perfect harmony between inner values and internalized law was perfect obedience. Out of this perfect obedience there came perfect freedom. In other words, Jesus was free to do spontaneously whatever he liked, because the value system which guided his preferences or desires was in perfect harmony with the law of unselfish love.

Jesus did not have to stop and ask himself in every situation what the law of God or the will of the Father was. It was in his heart so that he spontaneously and freely lived in it, knowing that what pleased him was always what would please the Father (John 8:29).

Here are the two covenants contrasted:

Old covenant	New covenant
(a) Sin merely covered	(a) Sin cleansed away
(b) External law on stone tablets	(b) Internal law on human hearts
(c) Inner values of the sinful nature (heart of stone)	(c) Inner values of the Spirit (heart of flesh)

The indwelling Holy Spirit

The motive of covenant is, as we have seen, the desire of God for a personal intimate relationship with human beings, but a holy God can have communion only with a holy people: *"Be holy, because I am holy"* (Leviticus 11:44–45; 1 Peter 1:16).

The Holy Spirit unites us to the life of Christ and by his indwelling:

1. **Imparts the active holiness of Christ to us.** This is his sanctifying work (2 Thessalonians 2:13; Romans 8:1–9).

2. **Gives us active access to the Father** (Ephesians 2:8).

3. **Teaches us the relationship of sonship or adoption** (Galatians 4:6; Romans 8:15–16), and

4. **Maintains and deepens our relationship with God,** so that we live to please him (1 Peter 1:2).

The result is the glorious liberty of the new covenant, also called by Paul, *"the glorious freedom of the children of God"* (Romans 8:21).

Now the Lord is the Spirit, and where the Spirit of the Lord is,
there is freedom. And we, who with unveiled faces all reflect the
Lord's glory, are being transformed into his likeness with ever-
increasing glory, which comes from the Lord, who is the Spirit.
                                        (2 Corinthians 3:17–18)

The new covenant of peace made in the blood of Jesus Christ
achieved the purpose of covenant. The alienation caused by sin
has been overcome, God and humankind have been reconciled
and it is now possible once again, and this time forever, for God
to be their God, the nations of the earth to be his people and
God to dwell in the midst of them.

In achieving this end, the new covenant gathers in, and both
includes and expands, all that is provided under the previous
covenants. We will turn to the significance of this in the next
chapter.

7

The covenants today

We have briefly traced the nature and history of the covenants between God and human beings, culminating in the new covenant of our Lord and Savior Jesus Christ. We now have to consider whether, and to what extent, the previous covenants are still in force, and specifically:

1. Which, if any, of the old covenant promises are ours to receive today?

2. Which, if any, of the old covenant obligations do we still have to fulfill today in order to enjoy the benefits?

The unity of the covenants

There has been a great deal of unnecessary misunderstanding of the covenants due to a failure to grasp their essential underlying unity. That is, that from beginning to end they have a common purpose, namely to bring people back to a relationship of personal intimacy with God. We find this aim expressed throughout scripture in the covenant formula: *"I will be their God, they will be my people and I will dwell in the midst of them."*

From this perspective, it will be seen that each of the covenants we have examined has this relational aspect at their heart, but lays stress on particular aspects.

■ **In the Abrahamic covenant, the emphasis is on grace and faith.** The promise was given to Abraham by grace (Galatians 3:18), and was received by faith (Romans 4:16–17). Abraham is supremely *"the man of faith"* (Galatians 3:9) and the *"father of all who believe"* (Romans 4:11).

■ **In the Mosaic covenant, the emphasis is on obedience** to the covenant requirements. God sets the terms and Israel's duty of obedience to the terms is called "keeping the covenant" (Exodus 19:5; Psalm 103:17–18).

■ **In the Davidic covenant with its focus on the kingdom**, the emphasis is on the all-embracing, societal and even creation-wide sweep of the covenant under the Messianic King (Isaiah 9:6–7).

■ **The new covenant deals with the dynamics of the covenant relationship** and the problems of sin and obedience through the atonement, the internalizing of the law of God and the gift of the Holy Spirit (Hebrews 8:10–12; Galatians 3:14).

Thus the covenants represent one expanding revelation that reaches its climax in the new covenant, which is both the fulfillment and the expansion of the covenants that went before. It is also the means whereby the covenant goal of a personal relationship between God and people is finally achieved.

Are the covenant promises ours today?

The evidence for the continuance of the covenant promises rests not only on the essential unity of the covenants, but also on the following:

■ **All the covenants are everlasting**, because that was stated as God's declared intention when they were established. Therefore, once the promises were made they became inviolable. Paul makes this clear in Galatians 3:15–17, when he writes concerning the old Abrahamic covenant, *"Just as no one can set aside or add to a human covenant that has been duly established, so it is in this case."*

The covenant benefits could be forfeited by disobedience or violating the conditions of the covenant, but God remained faithful to his word and the promises were available for any succeeding generations that fulfilled the conditions of faith and obedience.

■ **The nature of God's promises is immutable or unchangeable.** The writer to the Hebrews affirms this with reference to the covenant with Abraham confirmed with an oath. But then he links that to our present situation, saying that we have this same hope:

> *God did this so that, by two unchangeable things in which it is impossible for God to lie, we who have fled to take hold of the hope offered to us may be greatly encouraged. We have this hope as an anchor for the soul, firm and secure.* (Hebrews 6:18–19)

■ **Gentiles had formerly been** *"excluded from citizenship in Israel and foreigners to the covenants of the promise, without hope and without God in the world"* (Ephesians 2:12). But now in Christ Jesus we have been brought near and are *"no longer foreigners and aliens, but fellow citizens with God's people"* (Ephesians 2:13, 19). Thus **we inherit the covenants of promise** (note the plural), the Abrahamic, Mosaic and Davidic covenant promises.

> *If you belong to Christ, then you are Abraham's seed, and heirs according to the promise.*   (Galatians 3:29)

> *"I will give you the holy and sure blessings promised to David."*
> (Acts 13:34)

■ **All the covenant promises meet their fulfillment in the person of Jesus Christ,** the promised Seed and the Davidic King.

> *For I tell you that Christ has become a servant of the Jews on behalf of God's truth, to confirm the promises made to the patriarchs so that the Gentiles may glorify God for his mercy.*
> (Romans 15:8–9).

> *For no matter how many promises God has made, they are "Yes" in Christ Jesus. And so through him the "Amen" is spoken by us to the glory of God.*   (2 Corinthians 1:20)

■ **The covenanted mercies of the old covenant are repeated in the new covenant,** for example:

- *Spiritual blessings*: to the Hebrews *"the blessing"* was what gave the soul its life and vital power. It was synonymous with the presence of God (*"and God was with him"*) and is always associated with covenant, both the old (Genesis 12:3; Deuteronomy 28:3–14) and the new (Ephesians 1:3; Romans 15:29).

- *Healing*: The covenant with Israel contained promises that had particular reference to health, healing and disease (Exodus 15:26; 23:26; Deuteronomy 7:15; Proverbs 4:20–22; Psalm 91:3; 105:37). Healing figures in the prophecies of the new covenant (Isaiah 35:5–6; 42:6–7; 61:1; Malachi 4:2 etc.) and was in the ministry of Jesus declared to be the fulfillment of these prophecies (Matthew 8:16–17).

- *Blessing on families and children*: This was evident in the Old Testament references (Deuteronomy 28:4; Isaiah 59:21) and children are included in the blessings of the new covenant (Acts 2:39; Mark 10:14).

- *Victory over enemies*: The covenant included this (Deuteronomy 28:7; Isaiah 54:14–17), and it is continued in the new covenant (Revelation 12:11; 1 John 5:4; 1 Corinthians 15:57, etc.).

- *Material blessings*: This was part of the old covenant (Deuteronomy 28:8, 11–12). Similarly, the new covenant blessing holds out generosity as both the path to prosperity and the purpose of prosperity (2 Corinthians 9:6–15).

Therefore, we can affirm that all God's covenant promises remain in force for his covenant people. They are unchanging, immutable declarations of God's will and purpose and disposition towards his covenant people. They express what God is disposed to do and will do on the performance of the conditions set out in the covenant. If we fulfill the conditions, we can depend on God being faithful to his promises.

What covenant conditions apply today?

Although the covenant promises of God remain in force because they are everlasting, can the same be said of the covenant conditions? Clearly the covenants introduce obligations that the covenant parties are required to fulfill in order to receive the covenant benefits.

▶ *The fundamental covenant conditions remain what they have always been, that is, faith and obedience.*

Israel failed to enter into covenant rest because of unbelief and the rebellion and disobedience that resulted from that unbelief.

> *To whom did God swear that they would never enter his rest if not to those who disobeyed? So we see that they were not able to enter, because of their unbelief.* (Hebrews 3:18–19)

Unbelief and disobedience disqualifies us from the covenant blessings, just as they disqualified a whole generation of Israelites in the wilderness.

But covenant faith is not merely believing that a promise of God is for us to receive, like a sort of blank check on which we can put our name. It is believing in Christ, it is faith in the covenant God behind the promise, letting the outcome of our whole life and destiny go out of our hands into his. That is why it is inseparable from radical obedience to Christ the Lord.

> *"Anyone who loves father and mother more than me is not worthy of me; anyone who loves son or daughter more than me is not worthy of me. Those who do not take up their cross and follow me are not worthy of me."* (Matthew 10:37–38)

> *"Those who would come after me must deny themselves and take up their cross and follow me."* (Matthew 16:24)

Jesus is not advocating the abandonment of family ties, but is demanding that where there is a clash of loyalty between the claims of family and the covenant claims of discipleship, the latter takes precedence.

▶ *Some conditions of the old covenants are, however, declared to be for a temporary purpose and have been superseded by the new covenant.*

■ **The law,** as we have seen, was put in charge of us to lead us to Christ, so that we might be justified by faith (Galatians 3:24–25). What the law could not do, Christ did for us (Romans 8:3–4).

■ **The sacrificial system** of the Mosaic covenant and the regulations for worship in the tabernacle have been rendered obsolete by the new covenant (Hebrews 8:1–13). We have Jesus, the mediator of a better covenant founded on better promises. His blood is the blood of the eternal covenant (Hebrews 13:20).
Covenant is for those who fear the Lord, as the Psalmist says,

> *The Lord confides in those who fear him;*
> *he makes his covenant known to them.*   (Psalm 25:14)

To fear the Lord is, according to Deuteronomy, to keep his commandments, to walk in his ways, to listen to his voice, to cling to him, to love him and to serve him. For such people, the promises of God are like an open book.

8

Marriage as covenant

Because covenant is concerned with the personal relationship between God and people, it should be no surprise to find that the most intimate of human personal relationships, that is, marriage, also takes the form of a covenant.

> The LORD is acting as the witness between you and the wife of your youth, because you have broken faith with her, though she is your partner, the wife of your marriage covenant. Has not the LORD made them one? In flesh and spirit they are his. And why one? Because he was seeking godly offspring. So guard yourself in your spirit, and do not break faith with the wife of your youth.
> (Malachi 2:14–15)

In the Old Testament, the image of marriage is used to describe the covenant relationship between God and Israel. He is a husband to Israel (Jeremiah 31:32; Hosea 2:7), and married to the nation (Isaiah 62:4), but unfaithful Israel is an adulterous wife (Ezekiel 16:32; 23:1–21).

In the New Testament, the church is the bride of Christ (Ephesians 5:32) and the wife of the Lamb (Revelation 21:9). In fact, in his teaching on the one flesh of marriage in Ephesians 5:25–33, Paul coalesces the two images of the church as the bride of Christ and the Church as his body. First, husbands should love their wives as Christ loved the Church (verse 25). Second, husbands should love their wives as their own bodies (verse 28). Third, a man feeds and cares for his body as Christ does the Church which is his body (verses 19–30).

In this chapter, we will summarize the main applications of

the covenant principles we have been discussing to the covenant of marriage. It has to be said, though, that as far as Christian marriage is concerned, there is a radically new and transforming factor to be taken into account. Unfortunately it is rarely understood and therefore seldom experienced.

▶ *Because we live under the provisions of the new covenant, the provisions that apply to Christian marriage are also those of the new covenant.*

In other words, the cross of Jesus Christ, which effected the final reconciliation between God and people and provided the new covenant, also provides spiritual power for the covenant of marriage. We will discuss this in more detail later.

Covenant characteristics of marriage

Note the following characteristics of covenant that apply to the marriage relationship:

Marriage is a bonded relationship

Marriage is entered into by a solemn promise, confirmed with an oath or vow by which the parties call God to witness the binding nature of the commitment they have entered into with one another. The heart of the marriage relationship is, therefore, the bond of personal loyalty between husband and wife. Because of the vows the marriage covenant is:

- **Pre-eminent**, that is, it takes priority over all other obligations other than those we owe to God as our covenant Lord. All other human obligations are subordinated to those of the marriage relationship, including vocation, job, ministry and civic responsibilities.

- **Permanent**, that is, marriage is intended to be a life-long relationship between one man and one woman (Matthew 19:3).

- **Inviolable**, that is, it must not be broken or violated, and adultery or unfaithfulness to the marriage vows is, therefore, the most serious form of wrongdoing (Exodus 20:14;

Hebrews 13:4). Note, however, that there are other ways in which the wedding vows can be, and often are broken. That also is unfaithfulness and breaking covenant.

■ **The basis of marriage as covenant is grace.** Marriage must be founded on grace and will function successfully only on the basis of grace. In human terms, grace may be described as doing good to one another gratuitously, that is, with no strings attached. To say, "I will come half way if you come half way" is not grace, it is law. To say, "I have done my part, now you have to do your part" is not grace, it is works. Covenant will not function on the basis of works or law, but only on the basis of grace.

■ **In covenant, the stronger party voluntarily undertakes obligation toward the weaker party.** In the marriage covenant, the Bible clearly places the greater degree of responsibility on the husband. It is the man who is to *"leave his father and mother and be united to his wife"* (Genesis 2:24). The husband is the one who is commanded to love his wife and to give himself up for her *"as Christ loved the church and gave himself up for her"* (Ephesians 5:25). He is to be considerate to his wife and treat her with respect as the physically weaker partner and heir with him of the gracious gift of life (1 Peter 3:7).

The advantages of covenant

Covenant may at first glance seem an awesome obligation for us to live up to. But there are particular blessings built into covenant that are of inestimable advantage as far as marriage is concerned. When we see what they are, we realize some of the wisdom of God in making marriage a covenantal relationship.

Here are some important considerations:

1. **In covenant we have the security of making mistakes and learning from them.** Without the protection of covenant, the demands of a perfect performance to keep a relationship going would become unbearable.

2. **Covenant requires the discipline of working through problems**, and not taking the easy way out and merely opting out of the relationship if the going gets tough.

3. **Covenant keeps us secure during the emotional lows and humdrum periods** that come in every relationship. The obligation and commitment of covenant remain regardless of our feelings, and save us from judging the relationship solely from the view of feelings.

4. **Covenant also keeps us from infatuations** springing from sexual attractions, emotional love or the temptation of being in close proximity to someone. Our covenant vows have already determined what our behavior ought to be.

5. **Covenant leads us to discover that the ungiven self is the unfulfilled self.** It teaches us that fulfillment comes from giving ourselves to each other and not just from getting from each other.

6. **Covenant is realistic in that it recognizes our fallenness.** It recognizes the need for us to prove our trustworthiness by keeping our publicly made vows to each other.

7. **Finally, covenant rests ultimately in the righteousness (that is, covenant faithfulness) of God himself.** Jesus himself is the guarantee of the new covenant (Hebrews 7:22).

New covenant provisions for new covenant marriages

We come now to the specific provisions of the new covenant as they apply to the covenant of marriage, with particular reference to Jeremiah 31:31–34 and Ezekiel 36:25–28.

▶   *Covenant is entered into only by sacrifice.*

Christ has become the sacrifice for us, and by identification with his death and resurrection, we die to our sinful past and enter into a new, living relationship with God. But by the same sacrifice, we can enter into a covenant relationship with one another in marriage.

The implications for us are as follows:

• **We must die to any past relationships** with, and any past emotional attachments to members of the opposite sex that would be in conflict with our primary relationship with our partner. "Forsaking all others" as the marriage service says, we have become separated unto each other.

- **We henceforth renounce our right to live for our own self,** for our own personal desires and satisfaction of our self-centered needs.

- **We enter into a new life in which we live wholly for our marriage partner,** to meet their needs and see them fulfilled as persons. Henceforth, whatever happens and no matter what arises, we are committed always to be *for* each other. All we have and are, is for them and on their side in any circumstance.

▶ *Because the problem of sin has been dealt with in the new covenant, the damaging effects of wrongdoing in marriage can be overcome.*

■ **The new covenant provides for forgiveness,** which deals with the guilt of sin (Jeremiah 31:34), therefore, we have the ability to forgive one another.

> *Be kind and compassionate to one another, forgiving each other, just as in Christ God forgave you.* (Ephesians 4:32)

Forgiveness is releasing from blame or recriminations or punishment or revenge. It ends the matter because it says: "I will never mention this to you, to anyone else, or to myself ever again, it is forgiven."

■ **The new covenant also provides for cleansing** to deal with the stain of sin (Ezekiel 36:25). Because of this, the relationship can avoid the effects of wrongdoing that often leave a marriage spoiled and tarnished. It is possible for the marriage relationship to be kept as fresh and untainted as a blood-cleansed conscience, as we learn to continually *"walk in the light"* with one another (1 John 1:7).

▶ *Under the new covenant, the law of God is internalized – it is written on our hearts by the Holy Spirit* (Jeremiah 31:33; 2 Corinthians 3:3–6).

In exactly the same way as it happens with the new covenant, the law of God regarding marriage can be written on our hearts. This is the law of love, the law of faithfulness, the law of honor and the law of understanding and compassion. When that happens, the law becomes not a set of rules or standards of behavior to obey, nor even a set of principles to follow. It becomes *the inner motivation that shapes all our behavior towards one another.*

The gulf that used to exist between what we knew we ought to do and the motivation to actually do it, has been bridged, so that living by the law of love becomes a way of life.

Furthermore, we are given a heart of flesh for the previous heart of stone (Ezekiel 36:26) – *a new set of inner values that is in harmony with the law of God.*

We have all been programmed with false, misleading and sinful values from the world around us regarding marriage, sex, the roles of husband and wife, and so on. We can be freed from these inadequate and wrong values. Instead, we begin to see marriage from God's perspective and to appreciate the glory of his design in the marriage relationship.

▶   *We begin to experience the indwelling presence of the Holy Spirit* (Ezekiel 36:27).

He is resident not only in our individual lives, but also within the marriage relationship. He is the bond of our union.

> *Two are better than one, because they have a good return for their work: if they fall down, one can help the other up. But pity those who fall and have no friend to help them up! Also, if two lie down together, they will keep warm. But how can one keep warm alone? Though one may be overpowered, two can defend themselves. A cord of three strands is not quickly broken.*
>
> (Ecclesiastes 4:9–12)

In his book, *The Marriage Covenant*, Derek Prince points out that a rope of three strands, no more, no less, is the strongest that can be made, because each strand is in constant contact with the other two. In the marriage covenant, the Holy Spirit is the third person in the relationship, in continuous touch with the other two and keeping them in continuous touch with each other.

In such a position, *the Holy Spirit is able to monitor the quality of our relationship*, and if we are sensitive to his reactions, we will know unmistakably when things are not right between us. We will also sense his joy when we are walking in unity with one another.

The result is that *we can correct matters that need correction before they become major differences or conflicts*. In other words, the Holy Spirit wants to intervene at an early stage when matters can easily be rectified. He corrects us without crushing us and humbles us without humiliating us. Similarly, he encourages us without making us careless, and blesses us without making us proud.

▶ *True knowledge of the other becomes possible*
   (Jeremiah 31:34).

The purpose of covenant, personal intimate relationship, becomes wonderfully possible.

Covenant began in the garden of Eden when man and woman lived in perfect intimacy with each other, naked and unashamed, while also living in perfect intimacy with God. The new covenant restores what was lost by sin, so that we come back to something like the garden of Eden in our ability to disclose ourselves to each other and to receive each other.

Here, as elsewhere, we are touching areas of what the Bible rightly calls "mystery." Not a puzzle or a complicated riddle, but a category of spiritual and existential truth that is known only by experience and can only imperfectly be described or explained in words.

One of the main features that distinguish marriage from all other types of interpersonal relationships is that of becoming one flesh (Genesis 2:24). Henceforth, without losing their individual identity, husband and wife become a single unit to whom God reveals himself and his truths and in which both partners grow to maturity together.

Equality, mutuality and complementarity are the hallmarks of the relationship that God has designed for men and women to live together in marriage. That being so, where gross differences in growth, development or maturity persist in a relationship, the reason may well be that there has not been the true bonding that creates the *"one flesh"* of the marriage covenant.

▶ **Remembrance is important**

In Malachi 3:16 we read,

> *Then those who feared the LORD talked with each other, and the LORD listened and heard. A scroll of remembrance was written in his presence concerning those who feared the LORD and honored his name.*

We cannot underline sufficiently the importance of remembering, recalling and rehearsing to one another the works of the Lord in our lives, and consciously seeking to understand his revelation and his dealings with us. Time needs to be set apart for this on a regular basis.

In my own marriage, we have found that last thing at night before we go to sleep we talk through the events and the experiences of the day. Mistakes can be put right, the Lord's hand discerned and rejoiced in, and harmony reinforced or restored. If we go to sleep in peace, we wake in peace, and if we wake in peace, we can walk through the day in peace.

Entering into new covenant blessings

What do we do if we realize that we have insufficiently understood the relevance of the new covenant for our marriage and, therefore, have failed to experience its radical life-giving provisions? Here are the simple steps to renewal.

- **Deal honestly with areas of failure**, whether sins of commission or sins of omission. Allow the Holy Spirit to search your heart and the quality of your relationship. Ask for and give forgiveness to each other and ask God to forgive and cleanse you and your marriage (1 John 1:9).

- **Seek understanding of the realities of the new covenant** as far as your marriage is concerned. This requires prayerful reflection and pondering on the scriptures, so that the Holy

Spirit can give revelation, and the word becomes a *rhema* to you both.

- **Come to the cross**, so that through that sacrifice you can enter anew into covenant with one another. This involves reckoning Christ's death as yours and passing through that death to a new heart commitment of covenant with each other.

  Make your vows again in the presence of God, promising to love, serve, honor, trust and compassionately understand each other and to live wholly for each other.

- **Appropriate the realities of the new covenant** – in other words, *"count on them"* (Romans 6:11). Receive grace as the basis of your covenant, and the ability to forgive one another and forbear with one another.

- **Recognize the presence of the Holy Spirit** within you and within your marriage. Allow him to write the law of God on your heart. This writing will generally be very specific and when God writes a law on our hearts, our motivation changes. The internalized law will set us free and our conscience will become very responsive in that particular area of attitude or behavior.

If you have enjoyed this book and would like to help us to
send a copy of it and many other titles to needy pastors in the
Third World, please write for further information
or send your gift to:

**Sovereign World Trust
PO Box 777, Tonbridge
Kent TN11 0ZS
United Kingdom**

or to the **'Sovereign World'** distributor in your country.

Visit our website at **www.sovereign-world.org**
for a full range of Sovereign World books.